ASE9 PLAN

More than just a cookbook

Everyday Store Selections

A COMPLETE GUIDE TO MAKE YOUR OWN PLANTBASED RECIPES WITH AFFORDABLE HOLISTIC INGREDIENTS

Goddess Jalayah

Ase9 Plantbased Cookbook
Everyday Store Selections

A complete guide to make your own
Plantbased Recipies with affordable holistic
ingredients

By Goddess Jalayah

Copyright 2022
ISBN 979-8-8419-1549-2

Ase9 PlantBased Cookbook
Everyday Store Selections

For more information:
Contact Us:
Email Us: ase9info@gmail.com

Website:asenine.com

Facebook: Ase9@Ase9Affirmations

Instagram: Ase9@_asenine

Youtube: Ase9 Affirmationshttps://www.youtube.com/channel/UCGigBoaPRsQbdpKqAO0mm2A

I Dedicate this work of Art To my beautiful daughter,
Aubree (Amma).

You appeared in my dreams before you were born. You activated the warrior goddess within me. Thank you for choosing me. Keep your temple (mind, body, soul, spirit, environment, and aura) clean, and your heart light as a feather.

Love, Mom

ALL of the information in this cookbook is for entertainment purposes only. The statements made have not been regulated by the FDA. It is not intended to diagnose, treat, cure, or prevent any disease. All information presented is not meant as a substitue to information from your healthcare provider. Please consult with your healthcare practitioner prior to using any new products.

These items can be found at Whole Foods, Amazon, Trader Joe's, Farms, and Farmers Markets.

Please remember to read food labels on back of boxes and containers.

Table of Contents

About the Author .... p 7-8
Introduction .... p 9-10

Plant Based Recipes

Turnip Greens .... p 11-12
Mac & Cheese .... p 13-14
Russet Mashed Potatoes .... p 15-16
Southern Candid Yams .... p 17-18
Cornbread .... p 19-20
Cornbread Dressing .... p 21-22
Sweet Potato Pie .... p 23-24
Potato Salad .... p 25-26
Banana Pudding .... p 27-28
Fried "Chicken" Mushrooms .... p 29-30
Baked Spaghetti .... p 31-32
Meatballs .... p 33-34
Jackfruit Pot Roast .... p 35-36
Homemade Biscuits .... p 37-38
Purple Onion Soup .... p 39-40
Plant Based Burger .... p 41-42
Chickpea "Tuna" .... p 43-44
Avocado Toast .... p 45-46
Fried Plantians .... p 47-48
Wild Rice .... p 49-50
Homemade Gravy .... p 51-52
Fried Okra .... p 53-54
Dandellion Greens Salad .... p 55-56
Fried Banana Blossoms .... p 57-58
Salisbury "Mushroom" Steak .... p 59-60

Amazing Plant Based Resturant Selections .... p 61-63
Plant Based Options - Quick Meals .... p 64-67
Everyday Store Selections .... p 68-76
Life Decisions .... p 77
Body's Connection To Nature .... p 78
How To Grow Your Own Food .... p 79
    Hydroponic Garden .... p 80-81
    Outside Garden .... p 82-84
20 Wild plants you can Eat in theWilderness .... p 85
Did You Know .... p 86
Food AND Pregnancy .... p 87-88
Apothecary and Refrigerator Goals .... p 89-92
Dr. Sebi Nutritional Food List .... p 93-95
Notes .... p 96-100

About the Author

About the Author:

My name is Jalayah Jeff and I am the Owner and CEO of Ase9. I was born in Saint Louis, MO raised in Memphis, TN and currently reside in North Carolina.

I began my health and spiritual journey unconsciously in 2012, but consciously in 2019. After 1 year of going cold turkey with eliminating meat, dairy, soda, fast foods etc, I immediately began to notice improvement in my health and wellness. I started drinking all natural herbal tea, and my usual, heavy, and painful 7 day long periods shortened to 2-3 days of light spotting, and my mental health became clearer, and more focused.

I noticed that manifesting magick became easier. I also noticed that once my womb, body healed, my heart became lighter. I have been working in the medical field since 2016, and fell in love with birth work after having my daughter during the pandemic of 2020.

I am a certified Postpartum Doula, and Placenta Encapsulation Specialist. I feel there is a huge need in my community to assist mothers, and their families well into their 4th trimester, postpartum. The best teachers are still learning as students, hungry for knowledge. The healers have healed themselves, and are still healing.

Contact Us:Email Us: ase9info@gmail.com

Facebook: Ase9@Ase9Affirmations

Instagram: Ase9@_asenine

Youtube: Ase9 Affirmations
https://www.youtube.com/channel/UCGigBoaPRsQbdpKqAO0mm2A

Introduction

As Above So Below:

Avocados resemble a woman's womb/uterus.
Figs resemble a man's testicles/sperm.
Walnuts resemble your brain.
Bella mushrooms resemble your ear.
Trumpet mushrooms resembles a man's penis.
Ginger root resembles your stomach, and the list goes on.

You are nature! You want to eat that which you come from and reflect. Let food be thy medicine. In 2019 I watched the documentary "What the Health" on Netflix and began eating clean. Many people say that certain diseases such as high blood pressure, diabetes etc run in their family, when in fact poor eating habits, and illness producing foods does. Break that generational curse. Inherit generational health and wealth. Meditation became a daily ritual of mine. It gave me a cool head, and a clear mind to focus on what I needed to accomplish this lifetime, my purpose. I became aware of the lessons I needed to learn so that I can graduate to higher realms instead of reincarnating back to Earth to repeat them. We are essentially stars wrapped in skin. Spirits in a body. We get a new avatar each time. I want to keep my temple as healthy and high vibrating as possible. Nipsey Hussle's transition opened my eye, the seed was planted, and I learned who Dr. Sebi was.

This plant based cookbook is inspired by Dr. Sebi, and contains his approved nutritional food list, and recommended herbs list. He was one of the master elder teachers around the world on herbal holistic health. Through his teachings and lectures I was taught that all dis-ease and ailments start from excessive mucus in the body by mucus causing foods. Detoxing, fasting, a complete lifestyle change, and drinking 1 gallon of natural spring water daily will drastically improve overall health and wellness. You want to vibrate at the highest rate you can by eating life giving, non-GMO, organic, SEEDED* fruits, and veggies.

Eat your medicine. Eat to live. Cook with herbs. Meditation over medication. After I began feeding my temple life giving foods, using fluoride-free toothpaste, using aluminum-free key lime/coconut deodorant, doing yoga/sun salutations, drinking/bathing/foot soaking with herbs, journaling my dreams soon as I woke up, and acknowledging my highly elevated ancestors of benevolence and sovereignty, my life began to transform in a positive way on a cellular/dna level.

Introduction
As Above So Below:

Go outside more and become one with nature again.
Sun gaze/Sun bathe and get that natural Vitamin D.
Hug the trees.

The Sun, the Moon, and the stars are calling to reconnect with you. After eating fruits, and veggies place your seeds outside as an offering to Mother Earth instead of the trash. In this day and age just about everything in the grocery stores have been compromised so do your best with growing your own foods, supporting local farms, and farmers markets. Even though this cookbook is not 100% raw & alkaline, it is dairy-free, soy-free, meat-free, and a great start to help substitute ingredients in your favorite comfort meals while transitioning to a complete plant based lifestyle.

Teachers who have inspired me on my journey include "IamSurvivingVegan" Orisha Oshun, Brother Bobby Hemmitt(siriustimesmedia.com), Dick Gregory, Dr. Delbert Blair, Phil Valentine, Dr. Llaila Afrika, Sister Myra Moss, High Priestess Chielo, Mama Ella (Samorysherbs.com), King Simon Numerologer, Goddess Shala (divineselections.net) and her partner Sen Say Dwight Jolly, Brother C. Freeman El, "The Goddess Collection" Krystal Alkaline Doula and many others. You can find a lot of their work on YouTube.

The movie collection "Hidden Colors" is a great start. Discern African Proverbs in the bible. Take what resonates, and do away with what doesn't. Look in the mirror, speak LIFE, and positive affirmations over yourself and family daily. You are the highest of the high(John 10:34). The Book of Psalms, and the Book of Proverbs are gems. Your soul is primordial, and immortal. Eat to live.

Sending love, light, and healing.

Ase!

Turnip Greens & Jackfruit

Duration:
1 ½ HourServes: 8

Jack Fruit
BBQ
Sandwich

Turnip Greens

(Shredded jackfruit-also good on bbq sandwiches)

Duration:

1 ½ HourServes: 8

Ingredients:

10 pieces of shredded jackfruit

3 tablespoons Earth Balance Butter

1 chopped purple onion

1 pound of fresh chopped turnips

3 cups of veggie broth

1 teaspoon of sea salt

1 pinch of red pepper flakes

1 teaspoon onion powder

1 teaspoon pepper

1 chopped red pepper

Instructions: In a large stockpot melt butter. Sautee chopped onions, and red pepper until soft. Add in veggie broth overmedium-high heat. Add jackfruit. Simmer for 10-15 minutes. Add onion powder, sea salt, and cook until tender. Add soaked, and triple pre-washed, chopped greens and fry until they start to get darker, and wilt down. Pour in veggie broth and season with black pepper, and red pepper flakes. Reduce heat to low, cover, and simmer until greens are tender, about 1 hour. Stir and cover for another 15-20 minutes. Serve and enjoy.

Mac & Cheese

Duration: 1 Hour
Serves: 8

13

Mac & Cheese

Duration: 1 Hour
Serves: 8

Tabitha Brown Inspired Cheese Sauce:
½ cup of cooked/smashed butternut squash and 1 potato

Season to taste. In a pot on low to medium heat, melt 4 oz. of Earth Balance plant based butter, add 3-4 tablespoons of nutritional yeast, ¾ cup of Silk plant based yogurt, season to taste. Add 4 oz. each of plant based VioLife cheddar and mozzarella cheese shreds. Stir, and melt down thoroughly. Add 1 cup of veggie broth. Stir until consistency is creamy. Add cooked pasta, and mix well. Season to taste.

Ingredients:

8 ounces of Kamut pasta or Chickpea Elbow Macaroni Noodles

¼ cup of Earth Balance Butter

2 ½ tablespoons of Bob's Red Mill Chickpea Flour

3 cups of Planet Oat milk (or any plant based milk)

2 cups of shredded VioLife cheddar cheese & (diced cubes of cheese)

½ VioLife Parmesan cheese

2 tablespoons of Earth Balance butter

Instructions:

Preheat the oven to 350 degrees F (175 degrees C). Boil noodles, then drain. Melt plant based butter in a medium skillet over low heat. Gradually add plant based flour, whisking until well combined. Slowly pour in plant based milk, whisking constantly until smooth. Stir in cheeses, and cook over low heat until cheese is melted and the sauce is a little thick. Put macaroni in large casserole dish, and pour sauce over macaroni. Stir well. Melt plantbased butter in a skillet over medium heat. Add breadcrumbs and brown. Spread over the macaroni and cheese to cover. Bake in the preheated oven for 30 minutes. Serve and Enjoy.

Russet Mashed Potatoes

Duration: 45 Minutes
Serves: 6

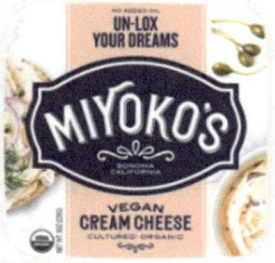

15

Russet Mashed Potatoes

Duration: 45 Minutes
Serves: 6

Ingredients:

1 bag of russet potatoes

1/3 cup of Silk Plant Based Heavy Crème

1/4 tablespoons of Earth Balance Butter

1 block of Miyikos plant based crème cheese

Salt & pepper

Veggie BrothBOU Brands LLC Veggie bouillon cube

Instructions:

Cut the potatoes. Peel your potatoes, and leave some of the skin on for extra nutrients and flavor. Cut your potatoes into evenly-sized chunks, about an inch or so thick. Transfer them to a large stockpot full of cold water until all of the potatoes are cut and ready to go. Boil the potatoes in veggie broth. Make sure that there is enough cold water in the pan so that the water line sits above the potatoes. Add 1 tablespoon sea salt to the water. Boil the potatoes for about 10-12 minutes until a folk inserted in the middle goes in firm with almost no resistance. Drain out all of the water. Whisk your heated butter, veggie cube, plant based milk and an additional 2 teaspoons of sea salt together in a small saucepan until the butter is melted. Set aside until ready to use. Pat dry potatoes. Mash the potatoes. Stir everything together. Pour half of the melted butter mixture over the potatoes, and fold it in with a whisk until potatoes have soaked up the liquid & all lumps are gone. Repeat with the remaining butter mixture. And then again with the cream cheese. Fold each addition in until combined to avoid over mixing, or else you will end up with gummy potatoes. Season to taste. Serve warm, and enjoy.

Southern Candid Yams

Duration: 45 Minutes
Serves: 5

Southern Candid Yams

Duration: 45 Minutes

Serves: 5

Ingredients:

5 medium sized sweet potatoes

8 tablespoons of Earth Balance butter

1 teaspoon ground cinnamon

½ teaspoon ground nutmeg

1 ¼ cup date sugar

1 tablespoon Simply Organic Vanilla Extract

Instructions:

Preheat oven to 350 F. Wash the sweet potatoes. Peel, then chop the sweet potatoes (in squares or circles) the thinner they are cut, the less time they take to get firm. Boil sweet potatoes for about 20 minutes then drain. Place the sweet potatoes into a bake dish. Place the butter into a medium sized pot, then melt it over medium heat. Once the butter is melted, sprinkle in date sugar, ground cinnamon, ground nutmeg. Turn the stove off, mix the ingredients, then add in the vanilla extract. Pour the candied mixture over the sweet potatoes, and coat all over. Cover the bake dish with foil, then bake the sweet potatoes in the oven for 30 minutes. Remove the sweet potatoes from the oven, and bake them with the remaining candied mixture. Cover the sweet potatoes, and bake them for another 15-20 minutes. Remove the sweet potatoes from the oven, and let them sit for about 10 minutes. Serve and enjoy.

Cornbread

Duration: 45 Minutes
Serves: 5

Cornbread

Duration: 45 Minutes

Serves: 5

Ingredients:

3 cups Bob's Red Mill Chickpea Flour

1 teaspoon Bob's Red Mill Baking Powder

1 cup Bob's Red Mill Corn Meal

1 ½ cup of date sugar 1 teaspoon sea salt

2 stick of softened Myioko's Butter

Sea salt

4 JUSTEgg replacement

2 ½ cups of Oat milk (or any plant based milk)

½ cup of Avocado oil

Instructions:

Combine the flour, baking powder, corn meal, sea salt, and date sugar in a large mixing bowl. Add the JUSTegg replacement, then pour in the oat milk. Add the Avocado oil and the butter. Mix everything until it's well combined. Fold the ingredients until well combined. Lightly oil a 9×13, and pour the cornbread batter. Bake on 350 for 35-40 minutes. Serve and enjoy.

Cornbread Dressing

Duration: 2 Hours
Serves: 5

Cornbread Dressing

Duration: 2 Hours
Serves: 5

Ingredients:

Cornbread enough to fill a 9×13
Rudi's spelt Bread crumbs and herbs

3-6 bunches of mashed burro bananas
(or JUSTegg replacement)
1 large diced yellow onion
1 gallon of Planet Oat milk (or any plant based milk)
2 1/2 teaspoon ground sage
2 tablespoon Earth Balance butter
4-6 cups veggie broth
14 oz. cream of veggie 14 oz. crème mushroom
2 teaspoon seasoning salt
1 teaspoon coarse black pepper Thyme
1 whole green, red, and yellow bell pepper
3 stalks of chopped celery
Good Thins Sea Salt and Pepper Crackers

Instructions: Start chopping, and dicing all of the celery, onions, and bell peppers. Also chop up the fresh sage. Drizzle the butter into a large pan, then place the pan over medium heat. Once the butter is nice and hot add in the onions, celery. Cook until nice and tender. Toss in the fresh sage. Continue to cook for 2 minutes. Turn the heat off. Crumble the cornbread into a large mixing bowl, along with the crackers. Add in cooked vegetables. Fold the ingredients until everything is well combined. Pour in the broth followed by the cream of mushroom soup. Add in the JUSTegg replacement, and mix everything until well combined. Sprinkle in the seasonings, thyme and pepper. Mix until well combined. Preheat the oven to 350 F. Lightly oil a 9×13 bake dish with avocado oil, then pour in the dressing mixture. Bake the dressing uncovered for about 45 minutes. Serve and enjoy.

Sweet Potato Pie

Duration: 45 Minutes
Serves: 6

23

Sweet Potato Pie

Duration: 45 minutes

Ingredients:
1 lb. sweet potatoes peeled & chopped
2 bunches of burro bananas

½ cup of Nature's Charm Evaporated Coconut Milk

1 tablespoon Simply Organic Vanilla Extract

1 tablespoon ground cinnamon
½ teaspoon ground nutmeg
¼ ground ginger
1 cup date sugar
8 tablespoons of softened Earth Balance
ButterPie Crust

Ingredients:
1 ¼ cup Bob's Red Mill Coconut Flour½ teaspoon of sea salt¼ cup cold Miyoko's oat milk. Sea salt butter diced or shredded¼ cup Earth Balance plant based shortening1 teaspoon of Simply Organic Vanilla Extract2 tablespoon date sugar1 ½ tablespoon ice spring waterInstructions:Sprinkle in 1 1/4 cup of Coconut flour into a large mixing bowl. Add in the cold butter, shortening, date sugar, salt, and of vanilla extract. Mix the ingredients until it forms into a dough, then wrap with plastic wrap and store the dough in the refrigerator. Toss the peeled and chopped sweet potatoes into a medium sized pot, and pour in about 4-6 cups of water. Place the pot over high heat, and boil the potatoes, until they are fork tender. Once the potatoes are done, drain the water, and let the potatoescool. Toss the cool sweet potatoes into a mixing bowl, and whisk until the potatoes are nice and creamy. Sprinkle in ground cinnamon, ground nutmeg, ground ginger, and date sugar. Add in egg replacement, evaporated milk, vanilla extract, and softened butter. Whisk until the mixture is nice creamy and airy. Remove the dough from the refrigerator, flatten it out, and then place it into a 9 inch pie pan. Bake the pie shell for 7-10 minutes on 325 F. Remove the shell from the oven, then turn the heat up to 350F. Add the sweet potato pie filling into the pie shell, and smooth it out. Bake the pie for 45 –50 minutes. Let the pie cool until it is room temperature. Serve and enjoy.

Potato Salad

Duration: 1 Hour
Serves: 10

25

Potato Salad

Duration: 1 Hour

Serves: 10

Ingredients:
2-½ pounds russet potatoes peeled and chopped
JUSTegg replacements
¼ cup Woodstock Sweet Relish
1 Chopped Purple Onion
¼ cup Simple Truth Organic Yellow Mustard
1 ½ cup Follow your Heart Plant based (Soy free) Mayo
½ teaspoon ground black pepper
1-½ teaspoon Simply Organic Seasoning Salt

Instructions:

Peel the potatoes, rinse under cool water. Chop the potatoes. Place the potatoes in a large pot. Add the JUSTegg. Boil the potatoes and applesauce separate. Pour in enough water to cover the potatoes and sauce. Place the pot on the burner, and boil on high for 10 to 12 minutes. Carefully remove the eggs. Boil the potatoes for an additional 5 minutes. Drain the potatoes. Let cool. While the potatoes are cooling, chop the onions and pour in egg replacement. Gently mash the potatoes into slightly smaller chunks. Fold the eggs into the potatoes. Fold in the onions, and relish. Add seasonings and gently fold in. Add mustard and mayonnaise, fold in. Cover the potato salad and chill for at least one hour. Serve and enjoy

Banana Pudding

Duration: 45 minutes

Serves: 6

DATE

27

Banana Pudding

Duration: 45 minutes
Serves: 6

Ingredients:

:½ cup Date Lady Date Sugar

1 1/8 tablespoon Bob's Red Mill Cornstarch

1 ½ cup Mooala Banana Milk or BananaWave Milk

2 lightly beaten JUSTegg replacements

1 teaspoon Simply Organic Vanilla Extract

5-8 bunches of Burro(baby) Bananas

Voortman Banana Wafers

Instructions:
In a small saucepan, combine the sugar, cornstarch and salt. Stir in milk until smooth. Cook and stir over medium-high heat until thickened and bubbly. Reduce heat to low; cook and stir for 2 minutes longer. Remove from the heat. Stir a small amount of hot filling into egg replacements; return all to the pan, stirring constantly. Bring to a gentle boil; cook and stir for 2 minutes. Remove fromthe heat; gently stir in vanilla. Cover and chill for 1 hour. Just before serving, fold in banana. Garnish with crushed banana wafers, and Almondmilk Ready Whip
Serve and enjoy.

Fried "Chicken" Mushrooms
Duration: 10-15 minutes
Serves: 4-5

Fried "Chicken" Mushroom

Duration: 10-15 minutes

Serves: 4-5

Ingredients:

Unsweetened Oat milk

Truff Hot Sauce

Onion Powder
Old Bay Seasoning
Tony's NO SALT Creole Seasoning
Black Pepper

Bob's Red Mill Chickpea Flour
Plantation
Avocado Oil

Instructions:

Wash and marinate oyster mushrooms overnight in plastic zip lock bag. Heat up Avocado Oil to prepare for frying. Take a second zip lock bag and halfway fill with flour. Season your flour. Completely coat a couple mushrooms at a time by mixing flour and mushrooms together. Placing a glove on is optional to reduce mess. Lightly squeeze mushrooms as you take them out of the flour to make sure flour sticks. Place them in hot oil to fry. Once browned take out and place on rack for remaining oil to drain. Sprinkle sea salt, and ground pepper on top.(Fried oyster mushroom sandwich made by @AlkanationEats)

Baked Spaghetti

Duration: 1 hour
Serves: 6

31

Baked Spaghetti

Duration: 1 hour
Serves: 6

Ingredients:

Plant Based Italian Field Roast sausage
or veggie "meat" pieces Bella Mushrooms
ZENB Pasta Sauce (or any plant based sauce)

Follow Your Heart Grated plant based Cheese
Can of Rotel
Purple Onion/Green Bell Pepper
Veggie BrothPasta Sauce
Basil/Chopped Parsley
Sea Salt
Good Karma plant based Sour Cream
Follow Your Heart Shredded Parmesan
VioLife Shredded Cheddar Cheese
VioLife Shredded Mozzarella CheeseTongs

Instructions:

Preheat oven to 375 degrees. Chop, sauté, and season veggies, mushrooms and chopped Italian Sausage in tomato soup or plantbased marinara sauce. Mix in veggie broth, more seasoning until browned, and tender. Add Rotel, pasta sauce, and whole Basil Leaf. Mix plant based meat sauce, and season to taste. Boil Spaghetti noodles in hot generously sea salted water, cook until tender and drain. In separate bowl, mix sour cream, season with parsley, and other herbs. Add shredded parmesan cheese. Grate cloves inside, and mix well. Lightly coat the bottom of a baking dish with the meat sauce. Add the remaining meat sauce to noodles, and use tongs to mix in well. Spread a layer of noodles evenlythen add a layer of cream mix, shredded mozzarella and cheddar cheese, more noodles, meat sauce, and topped with remaining cheese. Bake for about 25-30 minutes until golden brown. Garnish with fresh chopped Parsley, and grated cheese. Serve and enjoy.

Meatballs

Duration: 1 Hour
Serves: 6

33

Meatballs

Duration: 1 Hour
Serves: 6

Ingredients:
Fresh Parsley
Purple Onion
Veggie Burger Mix
Onion powder
Sea Salt /Pepper
Hamburger Seasoning
Myoko's plant based Scallion Cream Cheese
VioLife Shredded Cheese
Good Karma Sour cream
JUSTEgg Replacements
Shredded jackfruit
Marinara plant based Meat Sauce Or
Agave Louisiana Memphis Style BBQ Sauce
Simple Truth Grape Jelly
Date Sugar

Instructions:
Chop veggies, and grate thin pieces of onion into bowl. Crumble, ground, and season shredded jackfruit, and veggie burger meat. Add grated onion, parsley, cream cheese, sour cream, and shredded parmesan. Gloves are optional to reduce a mess. Mix together well. Add 2 JUSTegg replacements, and 3 cups of breadcrumbs. Mix well. Knead into 1 big ball. Lightly oil a sheet pan. Roll meat into desired shapes. Place, and line up meatballs onto sheet evenly. Sprinkle more hamburger seasoning on top. Place meatballs in 400 degree oven for 20 minutes. Simmer BBQ sauce, agave, and grape jelly on low heat. Whisk well. Add date sugar and whisk again. Once meatballs are done cooking, bathe them in either the marinara sauce or the BBQ sauce mixture. Coat all over. Simmer in a crock pot on low. Garnish with scallions. Serve and enjoy

Jackfruit Pot Roast

Duration: 1 Hour
Serves: 5

Jackfruit Pot Roast

Duration: 1 Hour
Serves: 5

Ingredients:

Purple Carrots
Celery
Red Potatoes

Sea Salt/Pepper
Onion Powder
Canned Jackfruit in Brine
Bob's Red Mill Chickpea Flour
Bob's Red Mill Cornstarch
Purple Onion
4 cups Veggie BrothRosemary
Spring water
Earth Balance Butter
Thyme
1 tablespoon Bionature Tomato Paste

Mushrooms

Instructions:

Clean all produce. Peel carrots, chop all veggies into large chunks, and set aside. Rinse, drain, and set aside jackfruit. Place butter in heated skillet. Brown your onions. Add broth, seasonings, tomato paste, and Jackfruit evenly then sprinkle a nice coat of flour on all sides. Sear on all sides to develop crust. Mix cornstarch and water to create a slurry mixture in a separate cup. Bring gravy upto a boil, and whisk in slurry mixture to thicken your gravy. Bring to a boil to desired consistency for about 30 minutes. Lower to a simmer. In a large baking dish add in all veggies. Pour jackfruit and gravy all over veggies and spread evenly. Place in the oven on 325 degrees for another 30 minutes. Jackfruit should easily shred with two forks once tender enough. Garnish with parsley. Serve and enjoy

Homemade Biscuits

Duration: 30 Minutes
Serves: 10

37

Homemade Biscuits

Duration: 30 Minutes
Serves: 10

Ingredients:

2 Cups of chickpea flour (or any plant based flour)

1 tablespoon of plant based baking soda

½ teaspoon of sea salt

½ cup of plant based shortening

¾ cup of cold oat milk (or any plant based milk)

Preheat oven to 450 degrees F (230 degrees C). In a large mixing bowl sift together flour, baking powder and salt.

Instru

Cut in shortening with fork or pastry blender until mixture resembles coarse crumbs. Pour milk into flour mixture while stirring with a fork. Mix in milk until dough is soft, moist and pulls away from the side of the bowl. Turn dough out onto a lightly floured surface and knead dough briefly, 5 to 7 times. Roll dough out into a 1/2 inch thick sheet and cut out biscuits with a floured cookie cutter. Press together unused dough and repeatrolling and cutting procedure. Place biscuits on ungreased baking sheets and bake in preheated oven until golden brown, about 10 minutes.

Serve and Enjoy.

Purple Onion Soup

Duration: 1 hour
Serves: 6

Purple Onion Soup

Duration: 1 hour

Serves: 6

Ingredients:

3 purple onions

1 gallon of natural spring water

Desired seasonings

Instructions:

Chop your onions, and place them in a large pot ofboiling spring water. Boil for about 20 to 30 minutes if not longer for stronger results. Season to taste. Let mixture sit and cool off before straining into a bowl. Serve and enjoy.

Plant-Based Burger

Duration: 30 minutes

Serves: 5

Plant-Based Burger

Duration: 30 minutes

Serves: 5

Ingredients:

Tri color diced peppers

Onions

Oats

Wild rice

Liquid smoke

Hamburger seasoning

Other assorted seasonings

Avocado Oil

Instructions:

Start by sautéing all veggies on low to medium heat. Place all cooked veggies and other ingredients into a food processor or Vitamix blender. Do not blend too thin. Make mixture thick, chunky enough to mold well into patties, meatballs, and sausages. Amazon sells a molder online. Freeze overnight. Heat up oil in skillet and fry, or grill. Dress them up, serve, and enjoy

Chickpea "Tuna"
Duration: 5 Minutes
Serves: 5

Chickpea "Tuna"
(1 of my absolute fav snacks, SO yummy)

Duration: 5 Minutes
Serves: 5

Ingredients:
1lb pack of Garbanzo beans
Follow Your Heart Mayo
Simple Truth Organic Yellow Mustard
Woodstock Organic Sweet Relish
Dill Crumbled Oceans Halo Seaweed
and/or Nori Kake Seaweed Seasoning
Sea Salt
Black pepper
Old Bay SeasoningOnion Powder

Instructions:
Soak Garbanzo beans overnight. Drain, and place inside blender and/or food processor. Blend to desired texture/consistency. Scoop into large bowl. Mix in mayo, mustard, relish, dill, seaweed, and other seasonings. Serve on spelt bread as sandwich, with rye crackers, or plain chips and enjoy.

Avocado Toast

Duration: 5 minutes
Serves: 1

Avocado Toast

Duration: 5 minutes

Serves: 1

Ingredients:

Rudi's Organic Spelt Bread

Avocados

Cherry Tomatoes

Red Pepper Flakes

Sea Salt

Instructions:

Cut Avocados in half and take out the seed (plant for yourself or throw it outside for Mother Nature). Dice and scoop out avocado and mash onto toasted Spelt bread. Top with diced cherry tomatoes. Sprinkle red pepper flakes, sea salt, and other desired seasoning on top. Serve and enjoy.

Fried Plantains

Duration: 20 Minute
Serves: 4

Fried Plantains

Duration: 20 Minutes

Serves: 4

Ingredients:

4 Ripe plantains

Hemp seed oil or Avocado Oil

Instructions:

Heat up oil. Take your bruised looking, ripe yellow plantains and chop both end pieces off. Peel the skins off. Cut pieces into desired shapes. Fry in nonstick skillet on low to medium heat. Turn and flip until both sides are evenly browned. Place on rack so remaining oil can drain. Serve and enjoy

Wild Rice

Duration: 30 minutes
Serves: 6

Wild Rice

Duration: 30 minutes

Serves: 6

Ingredients:

2 cups of Wild Rice

6 cups of natural spring water

Sea Salt

Instructions:

Wash and drain your wild rice really good. Put 6 cups of natural spring water in a large stock pot., and heat up to a boil. Add sea salt to boiling water. Once water is boiling, add rice in over medium to high heat and let cook for about 30 minutes. Stir occasionally to prevent sticking. Once done cooking down, remove pot from heat and let rest for 5 minutes to absorb excess water. Fork through. Season to taste. Serve and enjoy

Homemade Gravy

Duration: 1 Hour
Serves: 8

Homemade Gravy

Duration: 1 Hour
Serves: 8

Ingredients:

¼ Avocado Oil

¼ cup Bob's Red Mill chickpea flour

¼ cup Bob's Red Mill Cornstarch

4 cups of Pacific veggie broth

4 cups spring water

4 cups oat milk or any plant based milk

4 cups Silk plant based heavy cream

Purple Onion Soup

Instructions:

Sear, season, and combine veggie "meat" in pan with oil. Remove most of "meat" from pan leaving 4 tablespoons of "meat" juice, and drippings. Use spatula to scrape up any drippings stuck to the pan. Turn on medium to high heat. Stir quick with a wire whisk so flour evaporates. Let
the flour brown before adding liquid. Slowly add broth, spring water, milk, and cream to pan. Continue to whisk to dissolve the flour into a smooth liquid. Add in purple onion soup. Season to taste. Let gravy simmer, and thicken. Serve over top mashed potatoes, and/or Salisbury mushroom "steak" etc. Enjoy

Fried Okra

Duration: 1 Hour
Serves: 6

Fried Okra

Duration: 1 Hour
Serves: 6

Ingredients:
1 Pound fresh okra
1 ½ cups of Planet Oat milk
1 stick of Earth Balance Butter
1 cup Bob's Red Mill Chickpea Flour
½ cup LA Chicken Fry Mix
3 teaspoons sea sal
t¼ paprika
½ teaspoon pepper
Onion powder
Avocado Oil

Instructions:
Heat 3 inches of oil in a deep pot. Remove the stem ends off okra. Slice each okra into ¾ inch thick pieces. Make sure okra is patted dry to coat better and stick. Lesswet more batter will stick. Place okra in a bowl along with butter and Milk. Coat evenly. Place flour, cornmeal, sea salt, paprika, onion powder, and pepper in bowl. Toss to mix. Place each okra in flour mixture making sure it's coated evenly. Repeat thisprocess for remaining pieces. Fry for 3 minutes or until golden brown. Serve and enjoy

Dandelion Greens Salad

Duration: 15 minutes
Serves: 2

55

Dandelion Greens Salad

Duration: 15 minutes
Serves: 2
Ingredients:

Bunches of Dandelion Leaves

Avocado Oil or Hempseed Oil

Sea Salt

Black pepper

Tony's No Salt Creole Seasoning

Follow Your Heart Salad Dressing

Instructions:

Wash bunches of leaves in cold water 3 times or more until leaves are clean. Pat dry. Get a large mixing bowl and whisk together oil, and seasonings. Toss salad in mixture. You can sauté mushrooms and other veggies to put on top of your salad. Avocado to replace dressing or use Follow Your Heart plant based dressings. Serve and enjoy

DANDELION GREENS
DANDELION IS OFTEN THOUGHT OF AS A WEED. THEY SUPPORT DIGESTION, STRENGTHEN THE KIDNEY, LIVER, AND IMMUNE SYSTEM. THEY FIGHT CANCER, DIABETES, INFLAMMATION, AND HIGH CHOLESTEROL. DANDELIONS ARE RICH IN CALCIUM, IRON POTASSIUM, MAGNESIUM, PHOSPHORUS, COPPER, VITAMIN B6, C, THIAMIN, RIBOFLAVIN.

Fried "Fish" Banana Blossoms

Duration: 15 Minutes
Serves: 5

Fried Fish Banana Blossoms

Duration: 15 Minutes
Serves: 5

Ingredients:
Upton's Banana Blossoms and/or Tropics Banana Blossoms in can(WITH BRINE)
Bob's Red Mill Plantbased Cornmeal
Lousianna Lemon/Pepper Fish Fry
Bob's Red Mill Chickpea Flour
Onion Powder
Old bay Seasoning
Black Pepper
Tony's NO SALT Creole Seasoning
Ocean's Halo Seaweed and/or seaweed seasoning
Truff Hot Sauce
Avocado oil
Tongs

Instructions:
In a large mixing bowl take your banana blossoms and rinse them over with cold water. Add all your seasonings to taste. Crush your seaweed up and add as well. Add generous amount of hot sauce. Putting on a glove is optional to not cause a mess. Mix around together well to get everything to stick. Letting it sit to marinate for a while is recommended, but it is optional. Take a second large mixing bowl and add your cornameal,flour, and fish fry. Take each blossom, toss, and coat all around nicely. Squeeze them generously to get the breading to stick, and let out any excess liquid as you mold. Any mangeled, straggly pieces left you can also shape, mold, and fry up as well. Sit them on a plate, or rack to let breading sit into them well after coating. Deep fry each side until golden brown. Use tongs to get them out. Place on rack so any excess oil can drain off. Serve and enjoy. You can pair be themselves, or with plantbased spaghetti, and cheese bread (because YES down south spaghetti is a side dish LOL).

~Featured Recipe~
Salisbury Mushroom "Steak"

Duration: 1 Hour
Serves: 5

Salisbury Mushroom "Steak"

Duration: 1 Hour
Serves: 5

Ingredients:
Purple Onions
Sliced Bella Mushrooms
Veggie Burger Patties or Large Port Cap Mushrooms
2 teaspoons Primal Organic Ketchup
1 teaspoon Wizard's Organic Vegan Worcestershire Sauce
Cayenne Pepper
Smoked PaprikaTony's NO Salt Creole Seasoning
Progresso Parmesan bread Crumbs
Earth Balance butter
Avocado Oil
BOU Brands Veggie Bouillon cube
Tomato paste
3 tablespoons Bob's Red Mill Chickpea Flour
Veggie Broth
1 teaspoon Grace Browning
Silk Heavy Cream

Instructions:
Chop veggies, and set aside. Crumble in alarge mixing bowl mushrooms, jackfruit, and burger meat. Add sauce, ketchup, bouillon powder, and other seasonings. Gloves are optional to reduce mess. Mix thoroughly. Add half of breadcrumbs then add in 1 egg replacement lightly beaten. Add in second half of breadcrumbs. Mix thoroughly some more until in a firm ball. Put into the refrigerator for 30 minutes. Take meat/mushrooms out, and fry in skillet with butter and oil until a crust forms on both sides. Take meat/mushrooms out skillet, and sauté choppedveggies golden brown in remaining oil, butter, and season to taste. Add sprinkles of Worcestershire sauce, veggie cube, and tomato paste. Mix well. Add in flour and mix through well scrapping the drippings off the bottom. Add in veggie broth over top all veggies. Bring to a boil, and reduce to a simmer to thicken gravy. Add in browning, and mix well. Whisk in heavy cream to gravy. Add port caps /meat back into the gravy to cook in. Baste them all together. Plate "meat" together on top of mashed potatoes. Serve and enjoy

Amazing Plant-Based Restaurant Selections

Mediterranean Hummus, veggie sandwich on spelt bread & 10 veggie soup in bread bowl

Fried mushroom kabob by Mama Roots at Fountain of Roots

Mushroom/Jackfruit Mix
Perfect for tacos/lasagna/wraps

Veggie "Sloppy Joe"
with
VioLife plantbased cheese slice

Plant-Based Options - Quick Meals

64

Plant-Based Options - Quick Meals

65

Plant-Based Options - Quick Meals

66

Plant-Based Options - Quick Meals

Everyday Store Selections

ALKALINE FLOURS

GARBANZO **AMARANTH** **QUINOA**

SPELT **RYE** **KAMUT** **TEFF**

@ALKALINE_VEGAN_NEWS

68

Everyday Store Selections

Everyday Store Selections

70

Everyday Store Selections

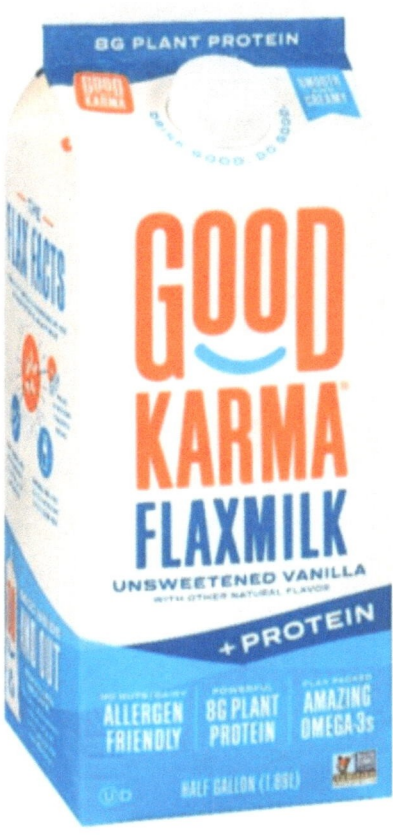

Everyday Store Selections

Everyday Store Selections

73

Everyday Store Selections

Everyday Store Selections

Everyday Store Selections

76

Better Health decisions are made before your food reaches the plate

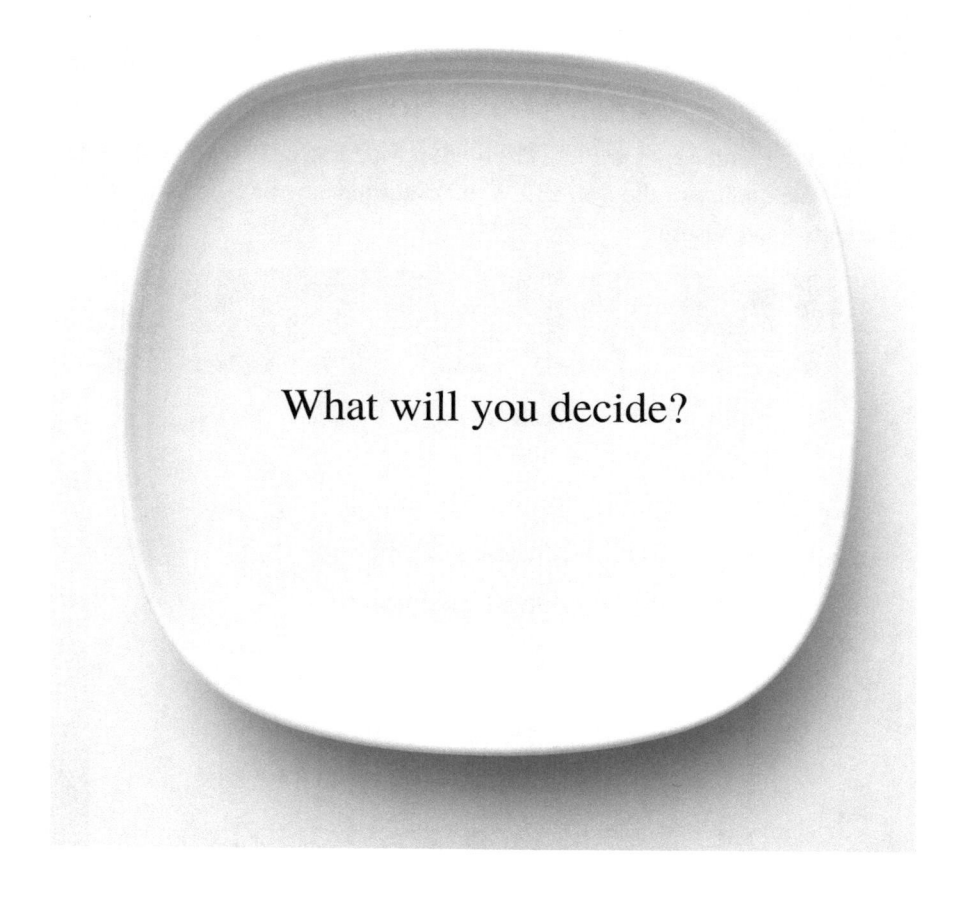

What will you decide?

The Body's Connection To Nature

It's no surprise that a diet filled with a variety of fruits and vegetables is an essential part of maximizing health. These plant-based ingredients are loaded with vitamins, minerals, antioxidants, fiber, and many other health-boosting compounds.

As Above So Below

The next several pages will cover growing food INSIDE or OUTSIDE the home. The quality of the Soil and Water determines your crop as well as nutrients you consume.

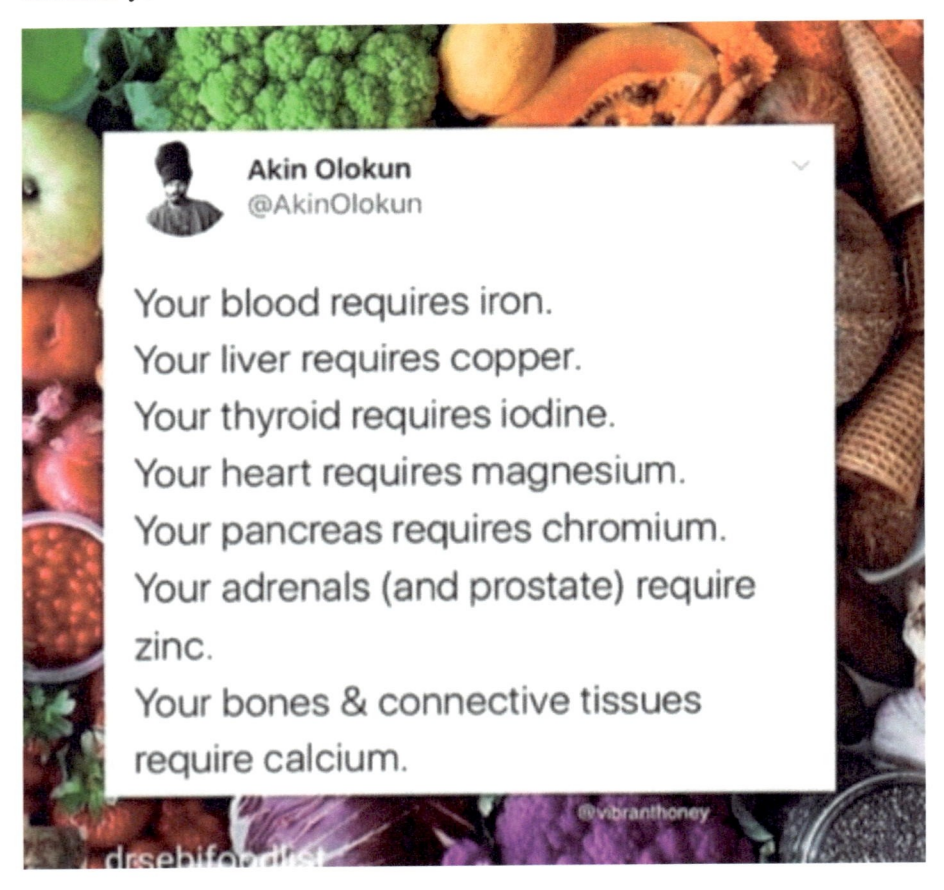

Akin Olokun
@AkinOlokun

Your blood requires iron.
Your liver requires copper.
Your thyroid requires iodine.
Your heart requires magnesium.
Your pancreas requires chromium.
Your adrenals (and prostate) require zinc.
Your bones & connective tissues require calcium.

How To Grow your Own Food

Hydroponic Vegetable Gardening

Hydroponic Vegetable Gardening

A hydroponic garden is a fun way to grow your own herbs and vegetables. Hydroponic systems use nutrient-enriched water instead of soil, and have existed for thousands of years. "Hydroponics" is a term derived from the Greek words for "water" and "working." Ancient Egyptians described growing plants in water, and the Aztecs used floating gardens called "chinampas" to grow vegetables.

A floating hydroponic garden is easy to build and can provide you with lots of nutritious vegetables. Best of all, this type of gardening avoids weeds and other pest problems common to soil-grown vegetables.

13 Easy Herbs to Grow Indoors
- Lemon Balm. Grow lemon balm plants for a single year for the best flavor
- Chives. Chives grow almost anywhere
- Mint. Growing mint indoors may be the best plan for most of us. ...
- Parsley
- Basil
- Cilantro
- Thyme
- Lemongrass

Best Plants to Grow Hydroponically
- Lettuce. Lettuce and other greens, like spinach and kale, may just be the most common vegetable grown in hydroponics.
- Tomatoes. Many types of tomatoes have been grown widely by hydroponic hobbyists and commercial growers.
  - Hot Peppers
  - Cucumbers
  - Green Beans
  - Basil
  - Strawberries

Fruits That Grow on Trees

Did you know that many fruits that grow on trees just happen to be the most popular? Some of the fruits that people like best grow on all kinds of trees around the world.

- Apples
- Pears
- Plums
- Peaches
- Citrus Fruits
- Pomegranates
- Cherries
- Figs

Vegetables That Grow Above Ground

Vegetables can grow both above-ground and below-ground, with different health benefits coming from the various types of vegetables. An above-ground vegetable is a plant with roots in the soil, and the leaves and vegetable harvest happen above the ground level. Examp

- Cabbage
- Zucchini
- Asparagus
- Kale
- Broccoli
- Cauliflower
- Cucumbers
- Bell peppers
- Brussels Sprouts
- Green Beans

82

Root Vegetables Grown Underground

Root vegetables grow underground, they contain high levels of nutrition that is gained from the soil. These vegetables are packed with vitamins and minerals, giving your body the vital building blocks needed to support overall health and wellness.

Root vegetables can be an essential part of a well-balanced diet, helping you reduce inflammation, lose weight, and prevent disease. The antioxidant properties of root vegetables are powerful for combatting free radical activity in the body, offering protection on a cellular level.

Root Vegetables
Vegetables grown underground:

- Yams
- Beets
- Parsnips
- Turnips
- Rutabagas
- Carrots
- Yuca
- Kohlrabi
- Onions
- Garlic
- Celery root (or celeriac)
- Horseradish
- Daikon,
- Turmeric
- Jicama
- Jerusalem artichokes
- Radishes
- Ginger

Root Vegetables Benefits

Research shows that root vegetables can play an influential role in protecting your health against various diseases, such as diabetes, cancer, obesity, heart disease, and more. The antioxidants and fiber in root vegetables help combat inflammation, which positively impacts overall health.

Many health conditions are associated with blood sugar issues, resulting from the Standard American Diet that includes a lot of refined carbohydrates. These unhealthy foods spike blood sugar and cause chronic inflammation – taking a toll on the body over time. On the other hand, root vegetables tend to be low on the glycemic index and cause less inflammatory issues than refined carbs and grains.

One of the benefits of root vegetables is that they can stay fresh for months if they are stored in the right conditions. For many years, people living in colder climates could harvest root vegetables in the fall, then have food to get through the harsh winter months by keeping root vegetables in the cellar.

20 WILD PLANTS YOU CAN EAT IN THE WILDERNESS

1. ASPARAGUS
2. LAMBSQUARTERS
3. BURDOCK
4. CHICORY
5. RED CLOVER
6. WILD GINGER
7. DANDELION
8. GREEN SEAWEED
9. KELP
10. AMERICAN ELDERBERRY
11. CATTAIL
12. WHITE MUSTARD
13. PRICKLY PEAR CACTUS
14. CHICKWEED
15. MINER'S LETTUCE
16. WILD ROSE
17. PINE NUTS
18. PURSLANE
19. BAMBOO
20. FIREWEED

DID YOU KNOW?

WHAT HAPPENS WHEN YOU EAT 2 SLICES OF ONIONS DAILY?

It helps increase immunity, treat depression, fight the common cold and flu being a potent natural antibiotic, and it helps you sleep better!

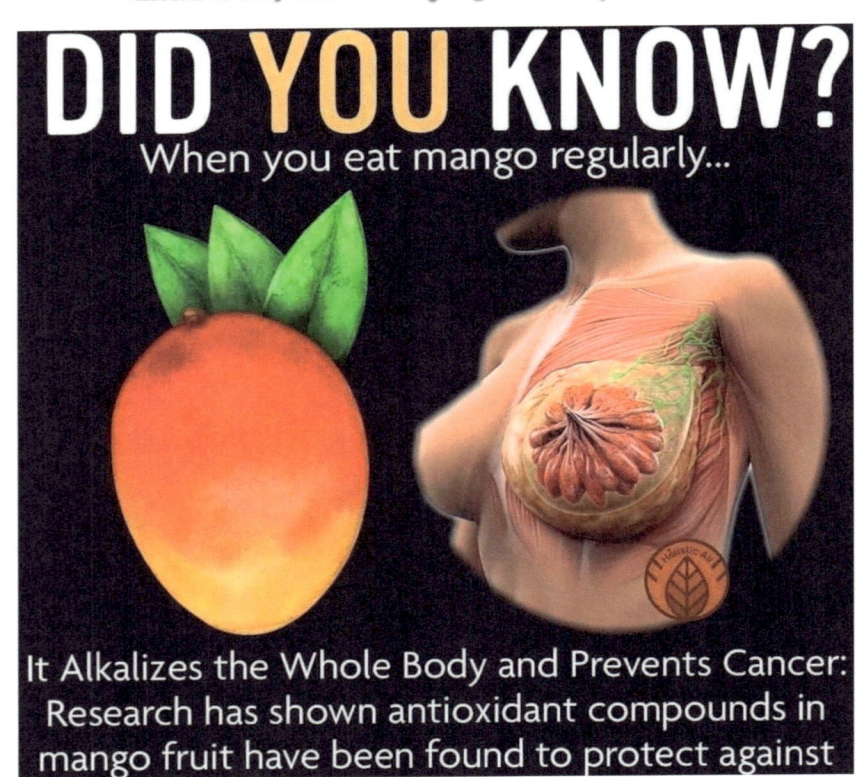

DID YOU KNOW?

When you eat mango regularly...

It Alkalizes the Whole Body and Prevents Cancer: Research has shown antioxidant compounds in mango fruit have been found to protect against

Food & Pregnancy

For pregnant and nursing Mothers
Please adhere to Dr.Sebi's recommened list when choosing foods from these pictures. Many of the foods within the book are hybrid, and are not recommended.

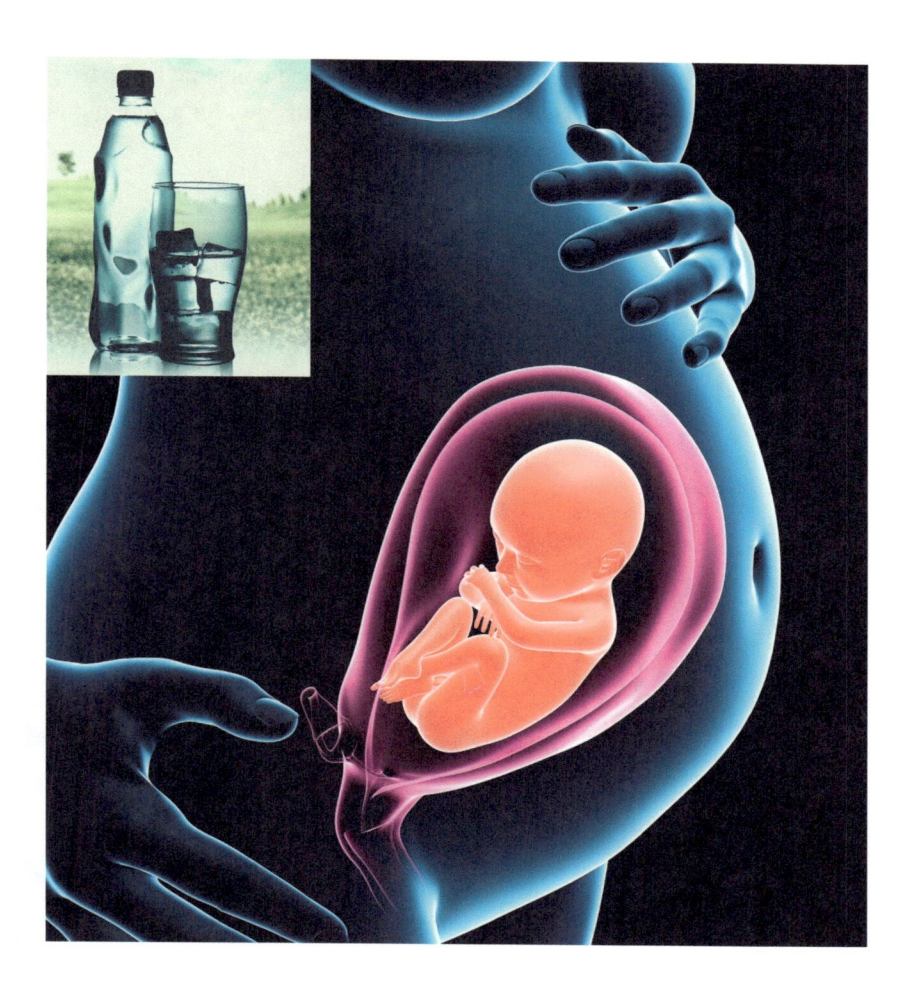

Pregnancy and Postpartum Care Recommendations:

1) Hire a doula at www.asenine.com
2) Go to regular appointments for mom and baby holistic chiropractic care during pregnancy, and postpartum.
3) Go to regular appointments for mom and baby massage therapy during pregnancy, and postpartum.
4) Sunbathe often for mom and baby.
5) Try everything in your power to eat healthier and consume herbs from www.asenine.com. Remember to keep stress levels low, for a high quality breastfeeding experience.

The more frequently the baby latches correctly, the more breastmilk you will produce.

Enjoy the Journey !

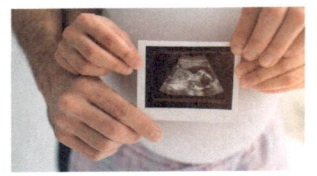

Apothecary and Refrigerator Goals

Your Health Is Your Wealth

Radial Geometry in Fruits
Formed by Mathematical Resonance

Fruit Combining

Sub-Acid
Fine with both sweet and acidic fruit

Acid
Don't digest well with sweet fruit.

Sweet
Don't digest well with acid fruit.

Melons
Digest super quickly. Do not mix with other fruit.

Fruits

- Apples
- Bananas (The smallest one or the Burro/midsize/original banana)
- Berries (All varieties, no cranberries)
- Elderberries (In any form)
- Cantaloupe
- Cherries
- Currants
- Dates
- Figs
- Grapes (Seeded)
- Limes (Key limes, with seeds)
- Mango
- Melons (Seeded)
- Orange (Seville or sour preferred, difficult to find)
- Papayas
- Peaches
- Pears
- Plums
- Prickly Pear (Cactus fruit)
- Prunes
- Raisins (Seeded)
- Soft Jelly Coconuts
- Soursops (Latin or West Indian markets)
- Tamarind

Vegetables

- Amaranth greens (Callaloo, a variety of greens)
- Avocado
- Bell Peppers
- Chayote (Mexican squash)
- Cucumber
- Dandelion greens
- Garbanzo beans
- Izote (Cactus flower/cactus leaf)
- Kale
- Lettuce (All, except Iceberg)
- Mushrooms (All, except Shitake)
- Nopales (Mexican cactus)
- Okra
- Olives
- Onions
- Sea Vegetables (Wakame/dulse/arame/hijiki/nori)
- Squash
- Tomato (Cherry and plum only)
- Tomatillo
- Turnip greens
- Zucchini
- Watercress
- Purslane (Verdolaga)
- Wild arugula

Nuts & Seeds
(Including Nut & Seed Butters)

- Hemp Seeds
- Raw Sesame Seeds
- Raw Sesame "Tahini" Butter
- Walnuts
- Brazil Nuts

Oils

- Olive Oil (Do not cook)
- Coconut Oil (Do not cook)
- Grapeseed Oil
- Sesame Oil
- Hempseed Oil
- Avocado Oil

Natural Herbal Teas

- Burdock
- Chamomile
- Elderberry
- Fennel
- Ginger
- Raspberry
- Tila

Grains

- Amaranth
- Fonio
- Kamut
- Quinoa
- Rye
- Spelt
- Tef
- Wild Rice

Spices & Seasonings

Mild Flavors

- Basil
- Bay leaf
- Cloves
- Dill
- Oregano
- Savory
- Sweet Basil
- Tarragon
- Thyme

Pungent & Spicy Flavors

- Achiote
- Cayenne/ African Bird Pepper
- Onion Powder
- Habanero
- Sage

Salty Flavors

- Pure Sea Salt
- Powdered Granulated Seaweed
- (Kelp/Dulse/Nori – has "sea taste")

Sweet Flavors

- Pure Agave Syrup (From cactus)
- Date Sugar

Important Things to Remember

- If a food is not listed in this Nutritional Guide, it is NOT recommend.
- Drink one gallon of natural spring water daily.
- Take Dr. Sebi's products one hour prior to pharmaceuticals.
- All of Dr. Sebi's products may be taken together with no interaction.
- Following the Nutritional Guide strictly and taking the products regularly, produces the best results with reversing disease.
- No animal products, no dairy, no fish, no hybrid foods and no alcohol.
- Natural growing grains are alkaline-based; it is recommended that you consume only the grains listed in the Nutritional Guide instead of wheat.
- Many of the grains listed in the Nutritional Guide are available as pastas, bread, flour or cereal and can be purchased at better health food stores.
- Dr. Sebi's products are still releasing therapeutic properties 14 days after being taken.
- Dr. Sebi says, "Avoid using a microwave, it will kill your food."
- Dr. Sebi says, "No canned or seedless fruits."

Dr. Sebi's Nutritional Food List

Herbs react differently from person to person. Please research each individual herb for your body makeup. Be sure herb selection coincides with any prescription drugs/ or OTC (Over the counter) medication. If you are TTC - trying to conceive or pregnant, consult your doctor before consumption.

- Anamu/Guinea Hen Weed-Whole Herb
- Arnica-Root, Flower
- Basil-Leaf, Essential Oil
- Bay leaves-Leaf
- Bladderwrack-Whole Herb
- Blue Vervain-Leaf, Flower
- Bugleweed-Aerial parts
- Burdock-Root
- Catnip-Aerial Parts
- Cancansa/Cansasa/Red Willow Bark-
- Cannabis (Marijuana/Hemp)-Flower, leaf, seed, stem
- Capadula-Bark, Root
- Cardo Santo/Blessed Thistle/Holy Thistle-Aerial Part
- Cascara Sagrada/Sacred Bark Bark
- Cayenne/African Bird Pepper-Fruit
- Centaury/Star Thistle/Knapweed-Flowering Aerial Parts
- Chamomile-Flower, Leaf
- Chaparro Amargo-Leaf, Branch
- Chickweed-Whole Herb
- Clove-Undeveloped Flower Bud

Dr. Sebi's Nutritional Food List (continued)

- Cocolmeca-Root
- Condurango-Vine, Bark
- Contribo/Birthwort-Root, Aerial Part
- Cordoncillo Negro-Bark
- Cuachalalate-Bark
- Dandelion-Root, Leaf (Mainly root used as medicine)
- Drago/Dracaeana Draco
- Dragon Tree-Leaf
- BarkElderberry-Berry
- FlowerEucalyptus-Leaf
- Eyebright-Aerial Parts
- Fennel-Seed
- Feverfew/Santa Maria-Whole Plant, Root, Flowering & Fruiting
- (Flor de Manita/Hand Flower Tree-Flower
- Blood Pressure Balance Tea)
- Ginger-Root
- Guaco/Mikania-Root
- Governadora/Chaparral-Leaf/Flower
- Hoodia Gordonii/Kalahari Cactus-Fleshy part of the stem
- Hombre Grande/Quassia/Bitter Wood-Bark
- Hortensia/Hydrangea-Dried Rhizome, Root
- Huereque/Wereke-Root
- Iboga-Root BarkKalawalla-Rhizome, Frond, Leaf
- Kinkeliba/Seh Haw-Leaf, Root and Bark
- Lavender-Flower, Leaves
- Lemon Verbena-Leaves, Flowering Top
- Lily of the Valley-FlowerLinden-Flower
- Lirio/Lily-Flower, Bulb, Leaf
- Locust-Bark
- Lupulo/Hops-Flower

Dr. Sebi's Nutritional Food List (continued)

- Manzo Root, Rhizome-Leaf
- Marula-Bark, Fruit, Leaf, Kernel, Nut
- Milk Thistle-Seed
- Mullein/Gordolobo-Flower, leaf, seed, stem
- Myrrh-Resin
- Nopal-Cactus
- Oak Bark /Encino-Bark
- Ortiga/Stinging Nettle-Leaf
- Pavana/Croton-Seed
- Pao Periera-Bark,Stem
- Palo Mulato-Bark
- Peony-Root, Root Bark
- Pinguicula/Butterwort-Leaf
- Prodigiosa/Bricklebush/Leaf of Life-Leaf
- Prunella Vulgaris / Self-Heal-Whole Herb
- Purslane/Verdolaga-Leaf Young Shoot, Stem
- Red Clover-Flower
- Red Raspberry-Leaf
- Rhubarb-Root
- Salsify/Goatsbeard/Oyster Plant-Root, Leaves,Flower, Seed, Young Stem
- San Pedro-Cactus
- Santa Maria/Sage-Leaf
- Sapo/Saponaire/Hierba del Sapo/Mexican Thistle-Whole Herb
- Sarsaparilla-Root
- Sea Moss-Seaweed
- Sempervivum/Houseleek-Leaf, Leaf Sap
- Sensitiva/Shameplant/Dead and Wake-Dried Whole Plant Root, Leaf, Seed
- Senecio/Groundsel/Ragwort-Whole Herb
- Shepherd's Purse-Whole Herb
- Shiny Bush Plant/Pepper Elder-Root, Aerial Part
- Tila/Linden-Flower
- Tronadora-Leaf, Stem
- Turnera/Damiana-Leaf
- Valeriana/Valerian-Root
- Yarrow/Queen Anne's Lace-Aerial Part Essential Oil

Store List / Meal Plans

Store List / Meal Plans

Store List / Meal Plans

Store List / Meal Plans

Store List / Meal Plans

Store List / Meal Plans

Made in the USA
Columbia, SC
25 July 2024